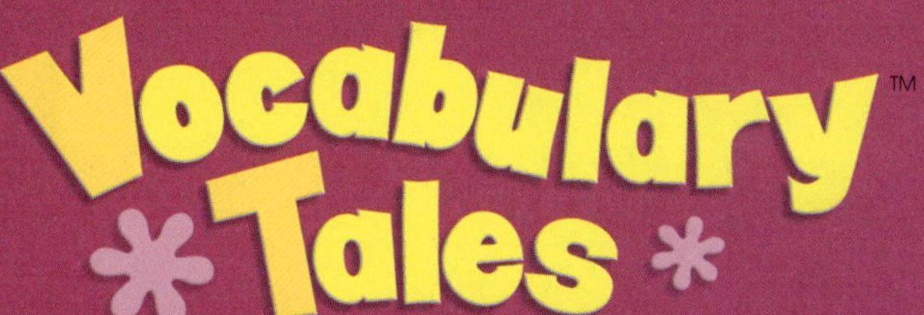

Callie Stays Up Late

by Carol Ghiglieri
illustrated by Paige Keiser

SCHOLASTIC INC.
New York • Toronto • London • Auckland • Sydney
Mexico City • New Delhi • Hong Kong • Buenos Aires

Designed by Maria Lilja
ISBN-13: 978-0-545-08860-2 • ISBN-10: 0-545-08860-7

First printing, January 2009

12 11 10 9 8 7 6 5 4 3 2 1 9 10 11 12 13 14/0

Building Vocabulary With This Book

This book contains eight key words that are important for all children to know. Read the story straight through for enjoyment. Then read it again, pausing to define and discuss each key word. Follow-up the tale with the fun activities on pages 14–16. When you're done, celebrate—kids will have added eight great words to their vocabularies!

Callie loved farm life. She loved her snug home. But sometimes she longed for adventure.

KEY WORD: second

Simple Definition: the smallest unit of time; 60 *seconds* make a minute

Sample Sentence: It took just one *second* for Erin to climb out of bed.

One night Callie was asleep when a scurrying sound woke her up. She opened her eyes. A **second** later, she saw a raccoon.

KEY WORD: nocturnal

Simple Definition: awake and busy at night

Sample Sentence: Bats fly out of their caves at night because they are *nocturnal.*

"What are you doing up?" Callie whispered. "I'm **nocturnal,**" he answered. "The middle of the night is when I eat and play."

KEY WORD: midnight

Simple Definition: twelve o'clock at night

Sample Sentence: When the clock struck *midnight*, Cinderella's carriage turned into a pumpkin.

"**Midnight** is amazing! It's a magical time to explore the world," said the raccoon. That gave Callie an idea.

KEY WORD: **week**

Simple Definition: seven days

Sample Sentence: It rained every day for a *week*, and then the sun came out.

The next day, Callie asked her pal Cora if she wanted to stay up late.

"We can go outside at midnight!" said Callie.

"No thanks," mooed Cora. "I've had a long **week**."

KEY WORD: **drowsy**

Simple Definition: sleepy

Sample Sentence: The long car ride home from her grandma's house made Cindy so *drowsy* that she fell asleep.

So Callie decided to ask Sammy. "Would you like to stay up late?" she said.

"Uh-uh," baahed Sammy. "I'd get way too **drowsy**."

“Polly, would you like to stay up late?” asked Callie.

“It sounds delightful, but I need my beauty sleep,” oinked the pretty pig.

KEY WORD: minute

Simple Definition: 60 seconds; there are 60 *minutes* in an hour

Sample Sentence: Kate scored a basket with only one *minute* left in the game.

“What about you, Harry?” asked Callie.
“Sorry,” he neighed. “I was planning on hitting the hay in one **minute**.”

KEY WORD: **dawn**

Simple Definition: the very beginning of the day

Sample Sentence: Tina woke up at *dawn* for the camping trip.

Callie wondered if Rocky the rooster would like to stay up late. But Rocky was already sound asleep. He had to be up at **dawn**.

KEY WORD: **hour**

Simple Definition: 60 minutes; there are 24 *hours* in a day

Sample Sentence: It took us an *hour* to walk around the lake.

"Oh well," thought Callie. "I guess I'll be staying up late all by myself."

Tick tock, tick tock. Callie watched the clock as each **hour** passed. At last, it was midnight.

Callie stepped outside. The moon was big and bright and beautiful.
"Wow!" thought Callie, "I wish I had some friends to share this magical night with."

And then . . . she did!

Meaning Match

time words

Listen to the definition. Then go to the WORD CHEST and find a vocabulary word that matches it.

1. seven days
2. the very beginning of the day
3. sleepy
4. sixty seconds
5. the smallest unit of time
6. awake and busy at night
7. sixty minutes
8. twelve o'clock at night

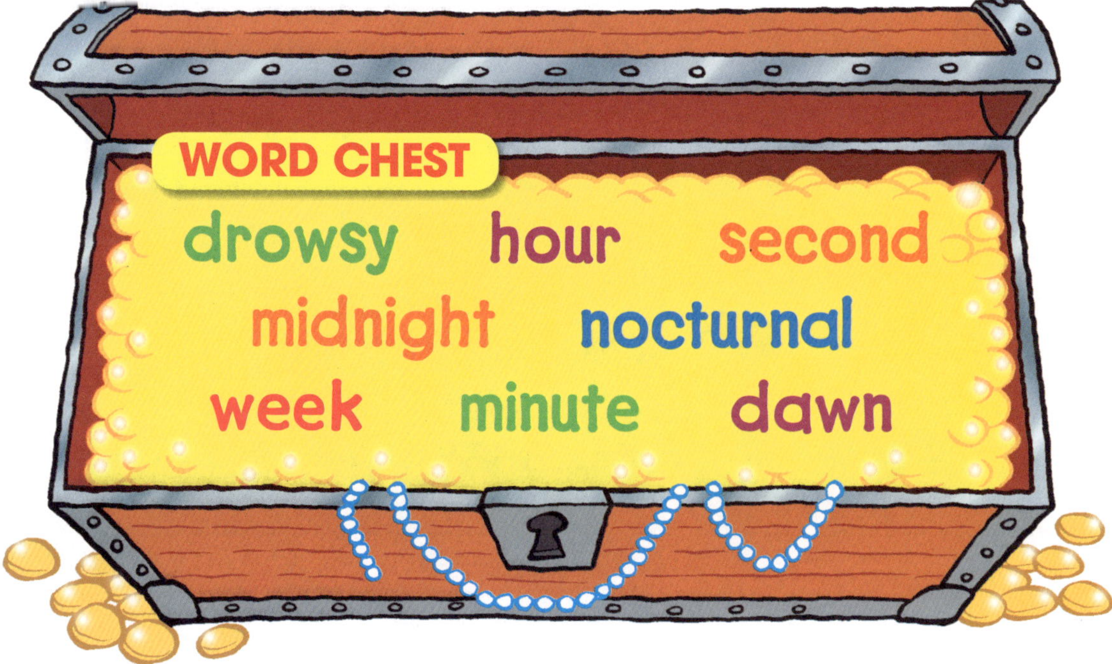

Answers: 1. week 2. dawn 3. drowsy 4. minute 5. second 6. nocturnal 7. hour 8. midnight

Vocabulary Fill-ins

time words

Listen to the sentence. Then go to the WORD BOX and find the best word to fill in the blank.

WORD BOX

dawn	drowsy	nocturnal	week
hour	second	midnight	minute

1. Michael woke up at ________ so he could see the sun rise.
2. Watching a movie late at night always makes me ________.
3. It takes just a ________ to snap your fingers.
4. There are 60 seconds in a ________.
5. Owls and raccoons are ________ animals.
6. That TV program is an ________ long.
7. My older brother stayed up until ________ on New Year's Eve.
8. When Sarah's grandmother visited for a ________, they did fun things for seven whole days.

Answers: 1. dawn 2. drowsy 3. second 4. minute 5. nocturnal 6. hour 7. midnight 8. week

Vocabulary Questions

time words

Listen to each question. Think about it. Then answer.

1. Have you ever gotten up at **dawn**? When? Why?
2. What can you do in one **minute**? Make a list!
3. If you could spend a **week** anywhere in the world, where would you go? Why would you go there?
4. Have you ever been awake at **midnight**? Tell about it.
5. If you had an **hour** to do anything you wanted, what would you do? Why?
6. Have you ever gotten **drowsy** and fallen asleep in a funny place? Talk about it.
7. Stand on one foot. How many **seconds** can you do it for?
8. If you were a **nocturnal** animal, what would you do at night?

Extra: Can you think of some more time words? Make a list.